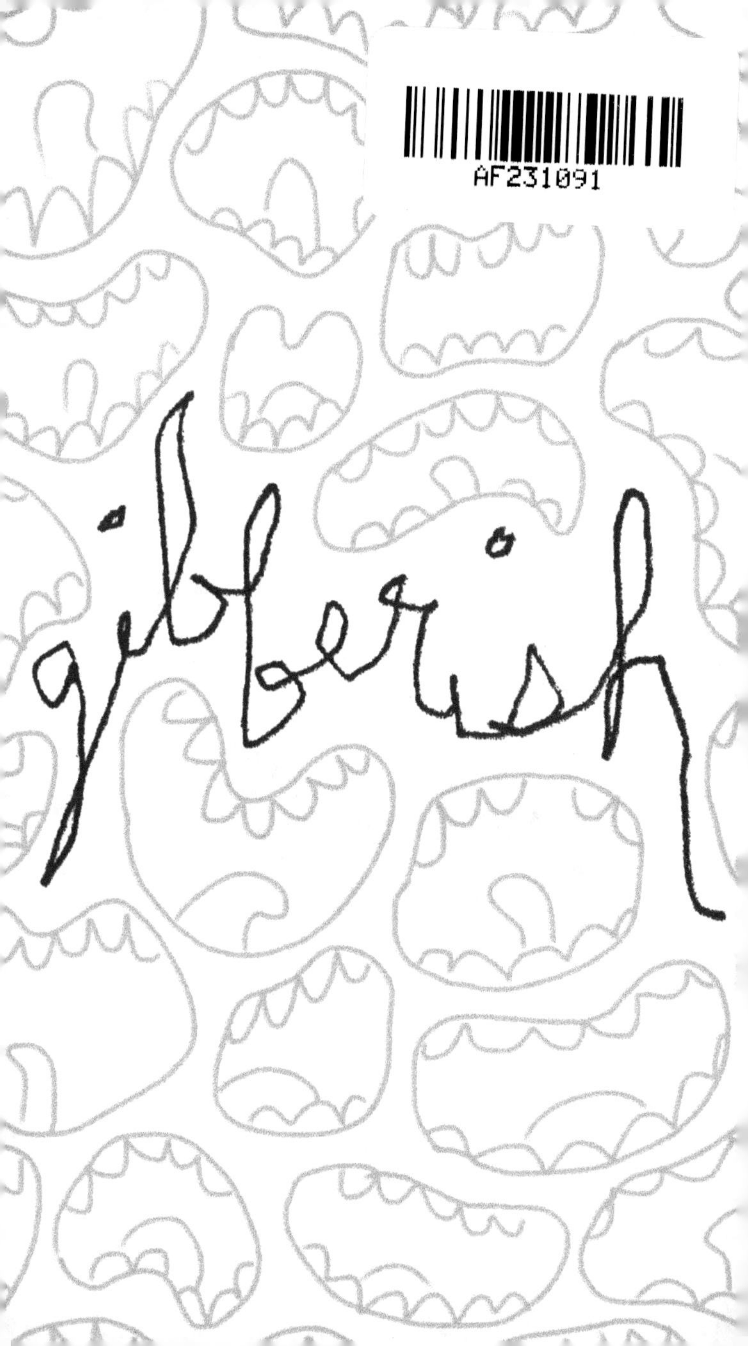
gibberish

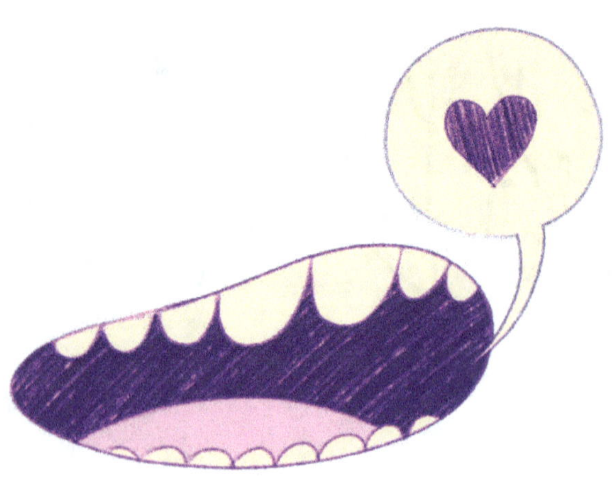

FOREWORD

While creating the cover, my main focus was visualizing the meaning of "gibberish" itself. *Gibberish* is messy, confusing, misunderstood, but something that we all recognize for what it is. There was a fine line between capturing the essence of the word as much as possible while maintaining the title's legibility.

After a few rounds of revision, I think the end result struck a perfect balance! Being an Asian American raised in two cultures under different names, I've had my fair share of "gibberish" moments as well.

That being said, I'm so thankful to *Lucky Jefferson* for giving me the opportunity to work on the cover of an issue full of poems that inspire and resonate with me!

KRISTINE PHAM
COVER ARTIST

ISBN 978-1-956076-01-1

GUEST EDITING by Ailun Shi
ISSUE DESIGN by NaBeela Washington
COVER ART by Kristine Pham

Ailun, pronounced like Allen, is a lover of books, calligraphy, and writing. She has worked with Empire & Great Jones Little Press, Helen: a literary magazine, and others. Learn more: ailunshi.wordpress.com

Kristine Pham is an Asian American artist at the University of the Arts in Philadelphia. Kristine's work: artkrisis.carrd.co.

Publication of *Lucky Jefferson* is made possible through community support.

Donate or submit to *Lucky Jefferson*:
luckyjefferson.com.

GIBBER JABBER

JOSEPH T. SALAZAR

KATHLEEN HELLEN

PAUL HOSTOVSKY

CAROL PARRIS KRAUSS

ELISABETH MEHL GREENE

MARISA LIN

EDYTHE RODRIGUEZ

JANE MUSCHENETZ

BABATUNDE ADESOKAN

SANDRA M. YEE

DEREK KANNEMEYER

ELLIOTT ORCHARD-BLOWEN

THETA PAVIS

MARK HAMMERSCHICK

MARIA S. PICONE

DIAN SEIDEL

SŁAWKA G. SCARSO

MAHAL KITA

We were fed prayers our entire lives
and that was supposed to be enough to toil
the fields, make love and dream.

But you know well enough
how the skin longs to be held
that even the cold snap of shrapnel
against the flesh bursts into musk
and frankincense as if somewhere
souls concede to irrational prayer,
and the god they worship is well-versed
in the inhumanity of desire and indecision.

From where I came from,
the weather is almost always a scorching
thirty-something celsius, so our pores
bare more before we could even undress.
Touch was omitted in lieu of sweet nothings,
shadows became bodies themselves
and their inaudible voices sang
the same hymns with enduring
devotion.

My ancestors shouted prayers believing
such words were easily forsaken
by a god who sits in his own rapture
as though he only chanced upon our land
wanting only followers and that he had
no hand in the bombs that explode
in our memories.

[continued]

No one lives to beg for mercy
and yet when our mouths are touched
by gunpowder, there is no recourse
but to pray and confront its bitter tang
as though we do not sleep naked with foolish
gods and that they have never ravaged us
to death.

If you want to say I love you
in my tongue, it has to feel like vespers
of old women who took their prayers
to the street:

Part-breakfast, part-devotion;
the whitewashing of a life massacred
by the police in the very pavement
where a life-sized statue of the Holy Mary
was left; rosaries swaying while arthritic fingers
expertly press on bead after bead as if
their worn skin could shelter the world
from another explosion.

JOSEPH T. SALAZAR *n.*

[JOH-SUHF] 1 THE ADDED ONE

HOLY CHRYSANTHEMUM

when i was born

    i bloomed

        into a

            chrysanthemum;

            the kind
            they make tea
            out of,

            the kind
            that gets
            capped
            in box tins
            & sent away.

when i was born

    i was shipped

                over

                      the Pacific

            to be shelved
             next to my loose-
            leafed cousins,

            all of us smiling
            down the aisle,

> people saying
> we were
> darling
> little things.

when i was sold

    my head

       was a tiny sun

        dropping

          into a ceramic mug,
        my petals unfurling
     in the heat, steam
releasing in curled wisps
    like pig's tails, wisps
        that whimpered
            in the naked air.

i learned it   first   in English:

chrysanthemum—

reciting the syllables like
catching myself on a stumble:

chry - *san*- *the-mum.* as in

[continued]

christen the baby   mumbling   in an airplane's   womb
        a damp   unravished blossom   face folded
        into a mother's armpit   tender stem
        peeling   out   over   the ocean to

San Francisco   the gold   gold country
        gold sun country country of golden sun
        where   my ancestors   once sung
        on the railroads broken souls worshiping

the theology of White white white everywhere in
        Minnesota there were people   good   kind people
        the good   kind of people but not the kind
        that understood   now

mum   as in mumma   dear mum   you cradled me
        on that flight   two blossoms softened
        by the tossing of the foreign wind
        from that day forward

you raised me   with a hope
that a name can be a protection   so
we chanted the other character
to make it true:

sheng zai sheng zai sheng zai you moaned at church
holy   holy   holy   i squawked at chapel

believing it could be a promise
or a prophecy dear mum only after
i had burst into a thousand fronds did i realize
you assigned me an impossible name—

for the preacher said to be holy
             is to be set apart
to keep oneself pure
for special purpose

                but how
                    can i be so
                         when i am cargo

                         to be clean
                              when the dirt
                                   so clings?

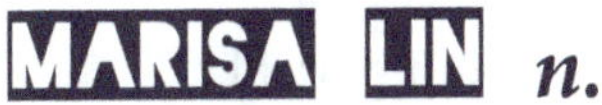

n.

[MAH-REE-SAH] 1 THE LITERAL TRANSLATION OF MY
CHINESE NAME CONSISTS OF TWO CHARACTERS THAT
TOGETHER TRANSLATE INTO "HOLY CHRYSANTHEMUM"

ELLIPTICAL TRAINING

For once I would like to play hard to get, love
                                    empty spaces

as in the gaps of bad translations, as in
                                       five people

in an exam room, Auntie
                    rubbing her stomach

with gnarled fingers, speaking
                      in Cantonese

to *Gong Gong, Gong Gong*
                          speaking

in Toisanese to me, me speaking
                      in English

to the American doctor and nurse, losing
                            half the words

along the way, then back around again
                            to address

Auntie's stools hardened by meds for arthritis.
                            See if you will

my multilingual pantomime of rectal pain
                            with nothing

to show for it. How can I give you

————————

[continued]

when since grade school I've striven
                              to make myself

clear? I don't recall what it was like to be fluent
                                    in my mother tongue—

how I knew putting food in my mouth was both
                                    hɛk and *eat*,

how the pages I read were both siː and *book*,
                                    how my tongue

could hold a language I couldn't read or write, the world
                                    a loose whole

before I divided my life into those who loved me and those
                                    whose ________

I desired, before *Hoo Hoo*'s story turned
                              into a weary recitation

of how I was once, in a strange country,
                        her closest friend.

鄧娟紅 (SANDRA M. YEE) *n.*

[ONG GUEN HONG] 1 GENTLE 2 PRETTY 3 RED

(TRILINGUAL) SIBLINGS

Family discussions: broken sentences
that start in one language,
morph into another,
constantly chasing the right word
as the drama grows

Secret languages spoken
not to be understood by parents,
neighbours, teachers, strangers.

An idiota* is an idiot§ is an idiota°
but your Babcia said it was a bad word *po Polsku*
so every quarrel would end
You're an idiota *po Polsku*

And even when your secret language
is half-forgotten, your brother will
be the only one to say your name just as it should be,

* in Italian
§ in English
° in Polish

– dad sometimes missing the point, and always the end.

– mum always telling you to behave twice as well.

– because truth flares in a nuance.

– to get your jokes before they're lost in translation.

SLAWKA G. SCARSO *n.*

[SWA–V–KAH] 1 GLORIA

WHAT FATHER MEANS

what father means when he names me
Baba-tun-de. it says a forebear returns
with the thud of a falling leaf. he comes
in the body of a boy. a thread follows
where the needle paves ways if the
pedigree is not bent, if the pedigree is
not crooked. The name seeks its bearer,
like humpback sticks through rains & ruins
but this boy wears the strengths of his fore-
fathers & his neck shall never be constricted
by any deadweight.

what father means when he shares me the
patronymic *Ade-so-kan.* It says a crown with
its diadem, with its garland, unites a compound
of names. a person who wears the crown beaded
with adulthood has outgrown child's play. he is the
one that blows the horn made of elephant tusk &
paves ways for others to pay homages to forebears
who planted the trees that currently shield us. & to
note that this crown unites all is to note that it is
a corncob that carries all kernels.

what father means when he christens me *Waliyu-llah.*
it says a man, who God favors: finds his father & finds
a crown. he leaves verses that kindle the altar. he
becomes a paladin *fi dini-Lahi* & a home that lamps
the planet.

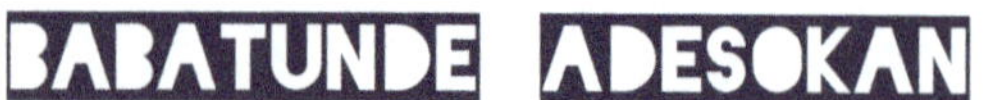

CLEAR & CRISP AS A SIP OF WATER FROM A MOUNTAIN CRICK

It all
began when momma's daddy rolled down a West Virginia gap,
& into a Carolina holler green with she-balsam and poverty.
He held purchase of just ten dollars & a poke of biscuits
soppin' in long sweetening.

Pa-paw
learned us to look twice at strangers & three times at kin.
We knew that what ailed us could be cured with granny's simples.
That being educated had nothing to do with how we sounded.
Intelligence has no ears.

Our twang
& turn of the word may sound odd to you. To us, our language
of Appalachia is lush & lyrical. We roll the letter r, as in we *warsh*
our car & all are master wordsmiths. We think our gibberish
is clear & crisp as a sip of water from a mountain crick.

CAROL PARRIS KRAUSS *n.*

[KAR-UHL] 1 CAROL IS A SONG OR FREE PERSON 2
THE SURNAME I WAS BORN WITH (PARRIS) MEANS ECCLE-
SIASTICAL LOYALTY.

OYO OMO ALAAFIN

When a town-crier sounds his gong.
Its jingles quicken & echo from tree
to tree. Breeze claps the leaves into
praise singing:

Oyo, Omo Alaafin
Ojo pa sekere Omo Atiba
Omo iku ti iku ko le pa
Omo arun ti arun ko le gbe de

It says: Oyo, the child of Alaafin
who traps
the pulse of words before they are
uttered, who impregnates the earth
with proverbs & presages warriors
with wisdom. who dares to forget a
home where lives the scion of
deities?

Oyo, the child of *Atiba* who beats
cowries into gourds, who strikes
sounds in the ears of heavens, thuds
the earth in leg-rhythms of *bata* & a
rhapsody of cadence

Oyo, the child of death who defies
mortality. the skin of living lion that
cannot be fashioned into a hunter's
hide. *Oyo* who strings morsels along
death's throat to stuff its stomach.

Oyo, the child of pestilence who unlaces
the ropes of sickliness, sprightly like
Olongo bird. Oyo, awash in bubbling
gbegiri & viscous *ewedu*, chews *pako*
into the eyes of ailment.

A *kin y'omo si le o* – we do not betray
our own, we forge them into men
through the crucibles of betrayals
& smiles.

Come to *Akesan* market, there, we sew
edges of our words into soft silks, suasive
psalms, & kazillion of *kawther*. For money
would not burden our neck but only heave
our pockets.

(Written for Oyo the ancient town of the Yoruba)

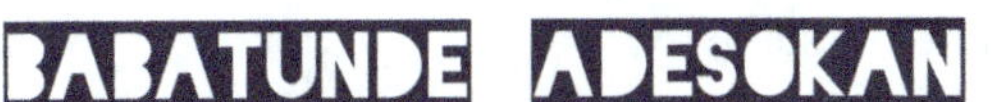

BABATUNDE ADESOKAN *n.*

[BAA-BUH-TOON-DEH] 1 A CROWN UNIFIES
2 BABATUNDE: THE RETURN OF A FATHER

SURVIVOR

half step
hunchback
shuffler
mover of mass
gazing vacant
into a slender
tumbler of Chicago water
as a vague sky forms
patterns
of barbed wire
excruciatingly white
bare knuckles
bearing violent scars
Nieder, runter,
jüdischer Bastard
wir werden schneiden
Finger weg
wenn du dich
nicht bewegst
cough
these eyes have seen
a forest
enchanted in ways
straight out of Warsaw
during the long crystal nights
when saturated soil
welcomed the night
these eyes have seen

[continued]

children
mothers
fathers
brothers
sisters
moving slowly
beyond the silence of roses
thorns bright
burning light
and yes there were Tigers
he sighs he coughs
stumbles into bed
his stone will read
Jerzy Wojtak
half step
hunchback
shuffler
mover of mass
Political Prisoner of
Auschwitz
Buchenwald
All in all
Just another brick in the wall

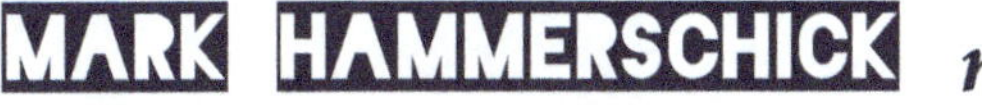

MARK HAMMERSCHICK *n.*

[MAHRK] **1** CONSECRATED TO THE GOD MARS
2 GOD OF WAR **3** WARLIKE

朝鮮姓名復舊令

조선 성명 복구령/**NAME REST⦿RATI⦿N ⦿RDER**

i.
in which the poet prays to her namesake

Ave, Maria, girl full of grace.
Thou, beloved, wished-for child, who crossed the transnational sea.

Blessed art thou among the children,
chosen from among our country's poorest lands.

Blessed is the fruit of thy virtual pen substitute, Microsoft Word,
showering with formatting woes these selfsame fruits.

Banished, outcast, and reviled, you will cover up the girl Ellen,
the plea of the suppliant child. Maria, girl of the oft-changing

name, reflecting our Western cultural institutions. Ill-fated
name, bitter name. Pray for us, at the hour of our death,

that we realize your rebellious nature
comes from our sins.

ii.
in which the poet obeys a request to 創氏改名 (창씨개명)*,*
create a surname and change your given name

two different names
I lived under
in the same country
Kim, commonplace, most Korean 김

ubiquitous as 김치
peppering the tables of every
family register, every family restaurant

피 코니 broke into this
wielding two uncommon consonants,
P for pillar holding up Greco-Roman
letters, K like the tines of 포크,
interpolating implement. long name
resonant like a tuning fork(u),
down up down. 마리아too
bookends with vowels, ah and i.
in the middle, there is always 수
consistency of being, Kim 수 Young,
Maria 수 Picone.

iii.

*in which the poet lists some epithets and nicknames belonging
to herself (incomplete)*

AJ
Adrienne/Adriana
shadowdancer9027
Ajantis Scipio
SooP
Maria from Korea
mpicone@_______.edu
Airam
mp15@______.edu
Maria-teacher
Soo Young
mspicone
"Maria Soo Picone, full of macaroni"

[continued]

iv.

in which the poet assembles her name from a list of possible meanings in 한자

I am the eternal hero. A perpetuity of glory. My river flows like a mirror, a projection of forever. I am an outstanding harvest. I gather water to myself for the flood. I shine in splendor, glorious reflection of a hero who gave himself to the flood, the river, the water. I am swimming in liquid. I am a movie that plays me at my bravest, that makes me the hero of the water. I am perpetually in flower. I swim in this river that waters the flowers. I reflect the river shining in the luxury of the palace with the cherry blossoms; I drift down that waterway to my destiny. I flood; I still have harvest outstanding. I am an echo, a projection. I am a river flower, a Narcissus. I am glorious. I am the river winding through Seoul. I am fluid and so is my fame, my splendor. Elegant, brave flowers always appear on the surface of the water. Swim deep; dive through the mirror to harvest the perpetual self. I am the eternal river, perpetuity of mirrors flowing forever, outstanding, glorious echo, projection of reflections, swimming deep in I, flooding, shining, liquid flower...

MARIA S. PICONE *n.*

[MUH—REE—UH] 1 SEA OF BITTERNESS 2 REBELLIOUS 3 BELOVED LOVE

ASL

What does it mean
that the thumb of this poem
drags its pink nail
down over the closed
mouth of this poem?
Is it in pain?
Can it not speak?
Is this prosodic
or phonemic,
this raised eyebrow
like a circumflex over
the I of this poem?
So far it only
questions itself.
It has a certain
manual dexterity,
but who can understand it?
Its face and its hands,
its tilted head,
its movement and invention,
its eye gaze (beautiful!),
the whole of its body
says it has passion,
but how will it persuade
with no voice?

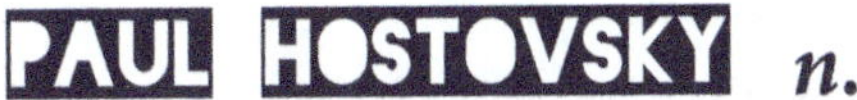

[PAWL] 1 HUMBLE 2 WHICH IS IRONIC BECAUSE
HUMILITY IS SOMETHING THAT HAS ELUDED ME MOST
OF MY LIFE.

ALL THE BAD GIRLS WEAR RUSSIAN ACCENTS

In the movies, villains have accents
sometimes German, but mostly Russian—
hard-edged lyrics of something forbidden,
severe haircuts, steel-blue eyes, and an appreciation
for Tchaikovsky, for a *Black Swan* kind of life,
for fairy tales built from curses

"Say something in Russian," the boys beg me in school,
hoping for death threats, nuclear arms codes or,
at least, a good cussword or two
I answer, "K-RA-SA-VEE-TZAH!"
a bullet through every consonant
bare my teeth on the "V" exhale over
that last "AH!" imply red lipstick

"What does it mean?" I don't tell them
only smile as they try to shape the unfamiliar with their mouths,
repeating my mangled conviction over and over, laughing

They will shout it after me, I know from experience,
throw it out with pride for remembering the next time they
see me maybe, even use it as an eternal greeting for
the only Russian-speaker they know

Which is why I don't teach them anything ugly
(it will only be poured back over me later
—a feedback loop quicker than some)
Krasaveetzah, in Russian, means *gorgeous woman*

Just like villains, tables can be turned

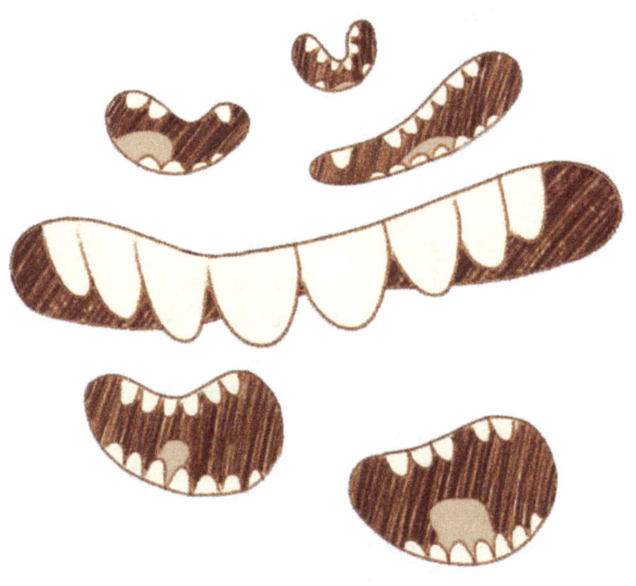

JANE MUSCHENETZ *n.*

[JEYN] **1** GRACIOUS **2** "JANE" WAS THE EASY TO PRONOUNCE VERSION OF MY RUSSIAN NAME THAT I CHOSE OVER "JENNY" WHEN I ARRIVED IN THE US EMIGRATION PROCESSING CENTER

3 MY 10 YEAR OLD SELF HAD SEEN ONE ENGLISH MOVIE WHERE THE BEAUTIFUL, STRONG-WILLED LEAD ACTRESS WAS NAMED "JANE", IT WAS THE MOST UNIQUE NAME I HAD EVER HEARD

REVOLUTION IS DISSENT

There are things to know and one of them is this:
inside me there is a secret part that answers only to
my middle name.

Reed, namesake of that which bends but does
not break. For all her faults look at this which my
my mother decreed; a daughter named Reed.

In the wet edge of a lake or marsh, the stiff, smooth stem
that reaches up above the muck. That which is revered.
That which is humble. That which is strong and sought

after. Hollow, circular, like my first name, but tough
fibrous, multi layered and so – not hollow or, hollow enough
to hold you and all the water, or all the breath being blown

through it. Reed. As in reader. As in first born daughter.
As in task taker. As in listener, my child's ear at the door
and under the table, like a reed to listen through, family

lore in murmurs coming to me. She gave me life and all my names
and by the time he met me I was formed and whole without
my father's name, but with his history. What part did she tell

[continued]

him? About the unbreakableness of the child or about my name's other meaning? That I was also named for Ten Days That Shook The World. For he who witnessed the revolution. For a hero, for a

dreamer, for John Reed, journalist, traveler, laid to rest at only 32. Destroyed by typhus and political heartache, laid to rest in the walls of the Kremlin. I aim to love life the way he did, with my arms open.

THETA PAVIS *n.*

[THEY-TUH] **1** THETA IS THE 8TH LETTER IN THE GREEK ALPHABET AND IN ANCIENT TIMES SYMBOLIZED DEATH **2** IT IS ALSO USED IN ADVANCED TRIGONOMETRY **3** MY MIDDLE NAME IS REED: I WAS NAMED AFTER THE REVOLUTIONARY JOHN REED

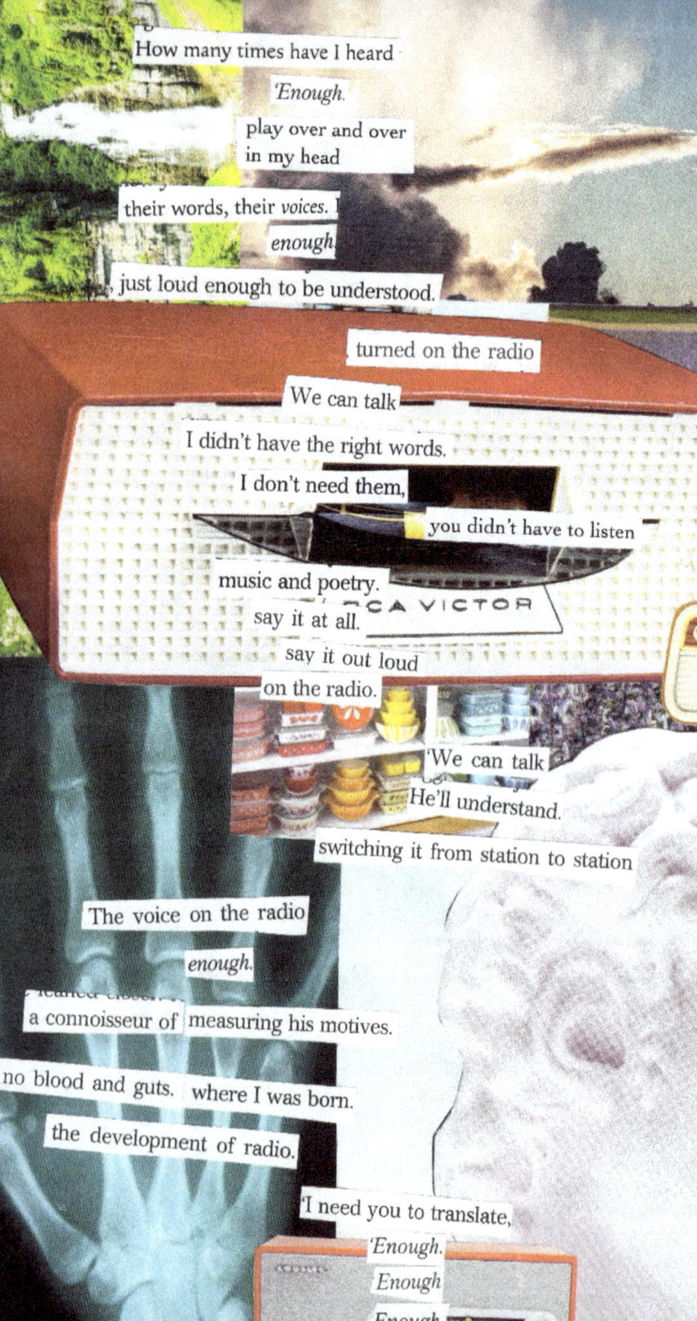

How many times have I heard
'Enough.
play over and over
in my head
their words, their voices.
enough
, just loud enough to be understood.
turned on the radio
We can talk
I didn't have the right words.
I don't need them,
you didn't have to listen
music and poetry.
say it at all.
say it out loud
on the radio.
CA VICTOR
'We can talk
He'll understand.
switching it from station to station
The voice on the radio
enough.
a connoisseur of measuring his motives.
no blood and guts. where I was born.
the development of radio.
'I need you to translate,
'Enough.
Enough
Enough

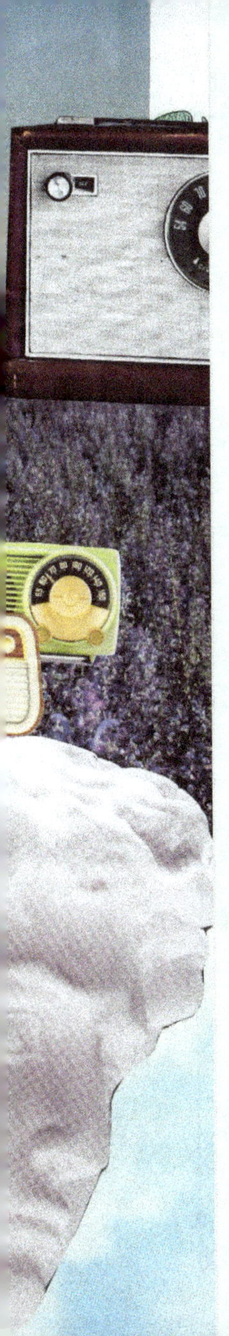

ELLIOTT
ORCHARD-BLOWEN

n. [EL-EE-UHT]

1 AN ENGLISH AND OLD FRENCH FORM OF THE NAME ELIJAH, MEANING "THE LORD IS MY GOD" 2 I CHOSE IT FOR PERSONAL SENTIMENTAL REASONS.

WORD BANK

po polsku
endangered language
nitnoy
sawatdee khrap/kha
moo ping
zhu ni shenti jiankang

wai
mapo tofu
krasavitsa
nieder
googly
heritage

mamaleh
buchenwald
ewedu
sheng zai
madrasa
solidarność

krymchak
haberdashery
polyglot
sospechoso
lespwa fè viv
culture
linguistics

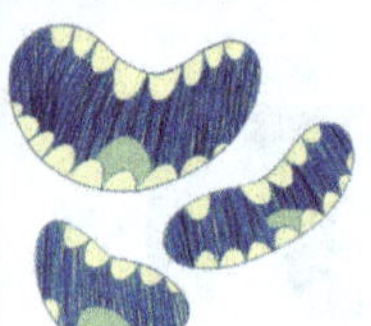

TEST YOUR KN⦿WLEDGE

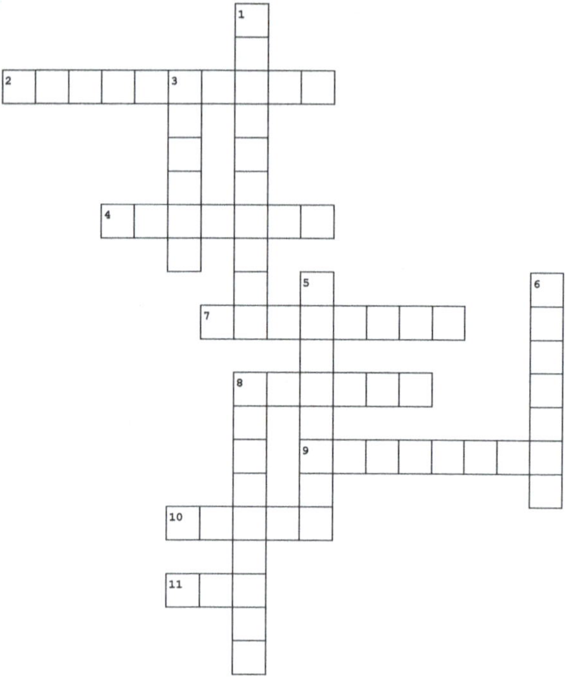

Across

2. one of the largest of the Nazi concentration camps established on German soil; "beech forest" in German
4. Thai Grilled Pork Skewers
7. a popular Sichuan dish including tofu
8. in the game of cricket, this refers to a type of delivery bowled by a right-arm leg spin bowler
9. means "hello" in Thai
10. also known as jute mallow, Egyptian spinach, bush okra; native to The Yoruba of Nigeria
11. a Thai greeting involving palms joined at the chest, head bowed; a way to express gratitude

Down

1. means "gorgeous" in Russian
3. means "a little bit" in Thai
5. the Polish phrase for "in Polish"
6. a Yiddish word that means "little mama"
8. the title of this issue; unintelligible or meaningless speech or writing

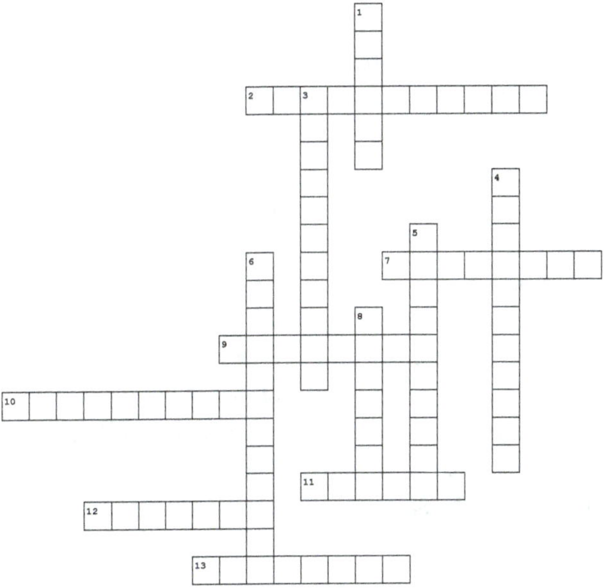

Across

2. the Polish word for "solidarity"
7. a person capable of speaking several languages
9. inherited traditions, monuments, objects, and culture
10. describes a language that is at risk of disappearing as its speakers die out or shift to speaking other languages; a language that is highly likely to become extinct
11. means "good morning" in Japanese
12. customs, arts, social institutions, and achievements of a particular nation, people, or other social group
13. an endangered language spoken by the Crimea people, a peninsula of Ukraine

Down

1. means "low" or "mean" in German
3. a Haitian proverb meaning "Hope Gives Life"
4. the science or study of language
5. means "suspicious" in Spanish
6. a men's clothing and accessory store
8. the Arabic word for "school"

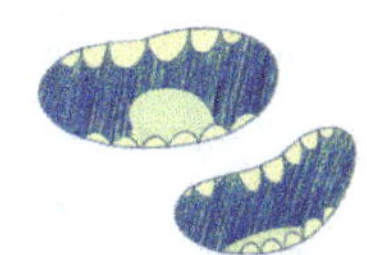

A LITTLE THAI LESSON

"Ne, neu, no. Nay, ner, noh. Neh, na, naw," they recite, almost in unison. She isn't 100% sure she's getting the nine Thai vowel sounds right, but she is 90% sure he isn't.

"Listen. Repeat after me," she says. Her lips progress from forced smile to fish face for the first three syllables, "Ne, neu, no."

"No, no, no." He crosses his forearms, making X's in rhythm with his words. They both know this bit of Thai body language. She orders her *pad thai* with shrimp. The cook crosses his arms—no shrimp tonight. He says they are going to the Skytrain. The cabbie crosses his index fingers—no, too far.

"It's pointless," he says. "We need to learn practical conversations, not practice unpronounceable vowels."

"Come on, a little effort," she says. "Please?"

"OK," he sighs, his thumb and forefinger an inch apart. "A *nitnoy* effort."

They run through the vowels twice, then she asks him if he's hungry. In Thai, it's "Do you want to eat rice?" which always makes her laugh. He is hungry, but he has never much liked rice.

[continued]

They fill their water bottles, leave their dusty, no-stove apartment, and wait on the gravelly shoulder for a break in the rush-hour traffic. This eight-lane highway and the skeletal dogs roaming roadside are Pathum Thani's greatest hazards, but there are no food vendors on their side of the road.

"*Sawahdee khrap*," and "*Sawahdee kha*," they say, almost in unison, as they make their *wais* and smile. The *wai*—palms joined at the chest, head bowed—and the smile are the other bits of body language they know. And love.

The cook says, "You speak Thai language, can!"

"*Nitnoy*," she replies. Sometimes *nitnoy* is enough.

They order. *Moo ping*, grilled pork, for him. He doesn't want the rice but doesn't know to say so. *Pad thai* with shrimp for her, but there's no shrimp tonight. X-X-X. The cook adds, in English, "You like spicy?"

"*Nitnoy*," she says again, then thank you, in Thai.

His *moo ping* arrives first, a bowlful of steaming rice topped with skewers of crispy pork.

"Go ahead," she says, "while it's still hot."

[continued]

Her *pad thai* is a glistening pile of noodles with bean sprouts, peanuts, tamarind sauce, and a wedge of lime. She digs in Thai-style—a fork in her left hand to load the spoon in her right—for a huge bite.

He looks up from his plate. "Drink," he commands, handing her a water bottle.

She digs an even huger spoonful of his perfectly plain white rice. She swallows, purses her lips, exhales a big breath, and wipes tears from her eyes.

"Too hot?" he says.

She clears her throat. "Tomorrow we practice *nitnoy.*"

DIAN SEIDEL *n.*

[DAHY-ANN] 1 DIAN IS A VARIANT OF DIANA, THE ROMAN GODDESS OF THE MOON AND THE HUNT 2 DIAN IS HOW SHAKESPEARE OCCASIONALLY SPELLED DIANA 3 IT'S HOW DIAN FOSSEY, THE FAMED BUT ILL-FATED FRIEND OF RWANDAN GORILLAS, SPELLED HER NAME

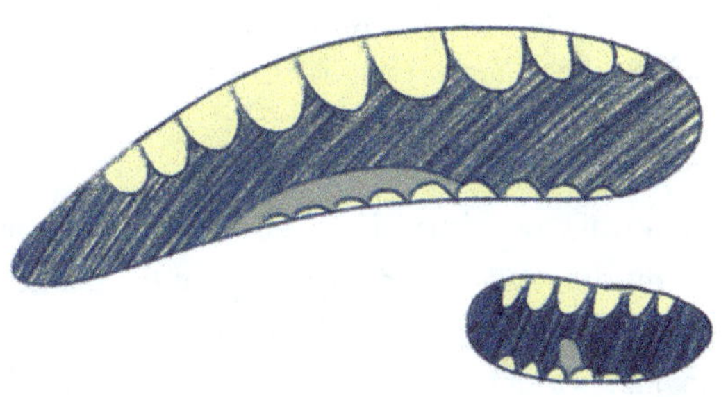

MY SKIN SPEAKS KREYÒL

M konn pale, it says. my mouth hears its name called and opens, throwing a wall between us. A laugh dances in your eyes now, you say my Kreyol is good (enough). I speak and the tasso price doubles.

My skin speaks bannann pressed flat, fried, and limesalted, speaks griyo fat crisped over this tongue. *Kòman w ye? M byen wi. E ou menm?   Kisa w ap etidye?   Yes   I am still in school. Yes   each day they teach me new ways to swallow this country.

My skin riffs over the shore in Okay, bathes in La Ravine du sud, trades goud for militon at the market. but my tongue says *I've dreamed of meeting you here, over this legum, this sòs pwa* / my tongue trades me for docked boats and other metaphors for failure / betrays me as always.

I whispersing Lanmou Fasil to Granma, she rasps my name through the barely-hit notes. *Ou konn pale Kreyòl?   On ti kras*, I confess. Granpa hears my stumbling, laughs at how I've stuffed his language into the roof of my mouth.

[continued]

Four months in, I have managed to lay my tongue flat just
so, fashion my mouth around the "r", the air gathering at
the top of my throat, then releasing: respire. Granpa guides
the rest, still ushering me across the border:

> *Unhook the vowels from your nose. You are not French
> / Stop coughing up your r's. No whistling in the house.
> Put more butter in the farine. If your epis is not good, it's
> downhill from there. Remove the piman if children will
> eat. Remove the pride from your eyes (there are things to
> learn here).*

My skin speaks to fanmi who I can only stutter back to, the
love somehow translating anyway. they ask and I always lie.
And they always let me   *Wi   M konn pale.*

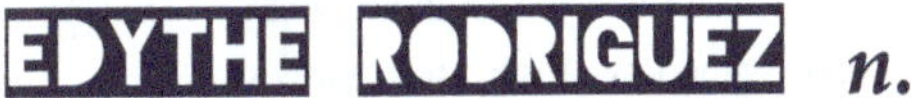

NISTLE

Nistle: a word that can form anagrams begun with each of its letters in turn.

(Acronym, from *nistle, inlets, silent, tinsel, listen, enlist.*)

"Eros," said the bookish girl, unbuttoning us, "is a *nistle.*
Eros, rose, ores, sore…" Kissing hello I'd offered her the rose,
but this ores, sore, *nistle* stuff had me flummoxed.
"Most *nistles*," she dirty-whispered, nose-nuzzling my ear,
nibbling and giggling a little, "are just three letters.
Own. Won. Now. Four letter nistles are juicier, though.
Like Eros. Longer and harder." I groaned—it was
hard to laugh. "*Ears. Arse. Sear* me. *Rase* me."

We tried it. I breathed in the sense and scents of her.
At her wrists, at her neck, strung silvers glinted, chimed.
My own, I said— *Now*, she said—
and for a while, in the guzzled dark's
shape-heaps and rased hungers, no words else sufficed.
But the while passed; the nistle failed to close.
We had loved, hurt, lost each other. The way one does.

Years later, when I looked up the word *nistle,*
I learned she had coined it, or mined it some place
my books didn't know to go. Only
on the turned leaf of my tongue could I find it—
where turning, chiming, in its ache and glint and gilt
of us, came tumbling this shadow-rinsed song—was she.

DEREK KANNEMEYER *n.*

[DER-IK] 1 KEEPER OF THE JARS 2 IT EXISTS IN HOLLAND BUT IS FUNDAMENTALLY AFRIKAANS 3 I'VE LIVED MOST OF MY LIFE IN COUNTRIES WHERE NO ONE ELSE AT ALL SHARES MY FAMILY NAME

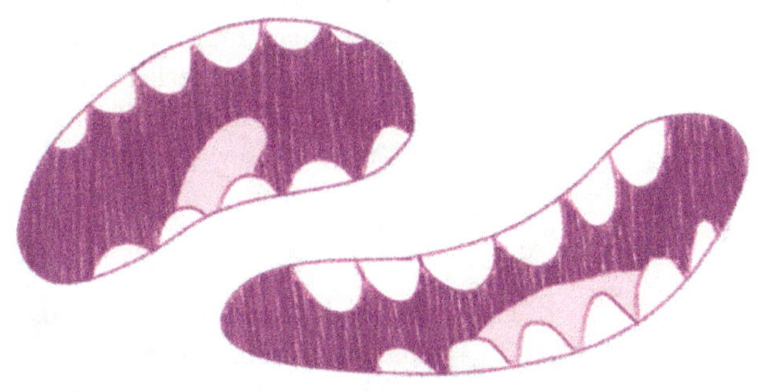

WATCHING QALB AL-ADALA[1] IN WEST VIRGINIA

باچر[2]

Under a striped blanket
in an Etihad seat
falling asleep upright
after notes of pre-flight prayer
chaa چ the chai sound[3]
kisses the Khor al-Maqta[4]
in my ear when they say
tomorrow

عدالة[5]

Subtitles float over sandy eyelids
in a state where Jim Justice governs
dream an alternate history
Gov. Adala of Firjinia al-Grebiyya[6]
who tweets of saving camel farms
and energy sustainability

أبو ظبي[7]

Abu Dhabi and Appalachia fuse
mingle steam from sautéed ramps[8]
with oud, cardamom and cloves
in my *dallah*[9] of Cordial Coffee,
the Sheikh Zayed bridge dunes
cascade over Shenandoah
and motorboats buzz
below the Grand Mosque
at Harper's Ferry

أكيد[10]

Perhaps alone in our neighborhood,

who else would yearn
for lemon-mint conversations
we spent five years
crisscrossing the Atlantic
to reach?

سافر[11]

Barely depart the state
anymore, once familiar with the touch
of distant tickets, paid for in weeks solo
stateside back then, now no airplanes at all
and scant moments to myself
when I visit Yas[12] at night
via Netflix

---

[1] 2017 series, (Arabic: Heart of Justice, English title: Justice), set in Abu Dhabi.

[2] Gulf Arabic: tomorrow.

[3] Ch-consonant, a sound unique to Gulf Arabic.

[4] Maqta Canal in Abu Dhabi.

[5] Arabic: justice.

[6] Arabic: Governor Justice, of West Virginia.

[7] Arabic: Abu Dhabi.

[8] A spring garlic variety native to West Virginia.

[9] Arabic coffee pot.

[10] Arabic: certainly.

[11] Arabic: to travel.

[12] Island in the city of Abu Dhabi.

ELISABETH MEHL GREENE *n.*

[IH–LIZ–UH–BUHTH] 1 DEDICATED TO GOD 2 FOLLOWS
THE GERMAN AND FRENCH SPELLING WITH AN S

DEAF HOUSE

My parents are deaf and I hate them. I hate them because they're deaf and because they never look when I call them unless I call them with my hands. They talk to me with their hands and I can't look away. Because looking away is rude, they say with their hands. It's a deaf thing, I guess, and I hate all the deaf things. Like the eyes that are always looking and the hands that say it's rude to look away, and the shoes that never excuse themselves, those deaf shoes. You can never tell the deaf shoes by their looks. You'd never think they were deaf until you heard them. Even a deaf man wouldn't think till he heard he wore deaf shoes. He'd walk through his house never guessing. Ring the doorbell, go ahead, you can tell the deaf house by the giant fireflies flashing their pear-shaped abdomens in every room. Every time the doorbell rings. Every time the telephone rings. So all the neighbors know. I hate the neighbors for knowing. And I hate the neighbors for telling me to tell my parents. Because the neighbors don't know the sign language. I don't hate the sign language, no, I hate the neighbors. For saying how beautiful the sign language is. And how lucky I am for knowing it. When they don't even know what they're saying. When they don't even know it themselves. And I hate my parents for not knowing what they don't know.

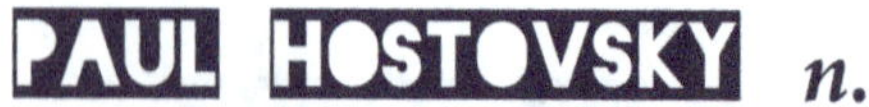

PAUL HOSTOVSKY *n.*

[PAWL] **1** HUMBLE **2** WHICH IS IRONIC BECAUSE HUMILITY IS SOMETHING THAT HAS ELUDED ME MOST OF MY LIFE.

SHARING THE PEAR 分梨

In Chinese, the pear is pronounced "li," but when translated to
English, it also means "separate." — The USC Digital Folklore Archives

When I brought it home, placed it on the counter wrapped in
mesh, it was a gift, individual,

not a spot of scald, never touched by any other woman
who is reaching at the market

for something rare. I know, you couldn't help yourself.

KATHLEEN HELLEN *n.*

[KATH-LEEN] 1 IN JAPANESE MY NAME IS "NEKO"
2 "KATHLEEN" WAS PROBABLY AN AMERICANIZATION
OF THE JAPANESE WORD FOR "CAT"

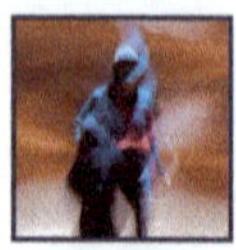

Sandra M. Yee (鄧娟紅) had to ask her mother how to pronounce her Chinese name. She lives in Phoenix, Arizona, where she enjoys hiking, camping, and thrifting for party frocks. Her work has appeared or is forthcoming in Bookends Review, Crazyhorse, Indiana Review, Rattle, and TriQuarterly.

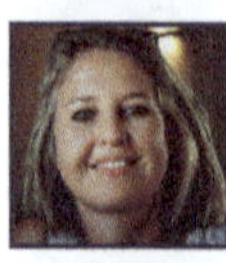

Sławka G. Scarso has published several books in Italy and works as a copywriter and translator. Her short fiction has appeared in Mslexia, Ellipsis Zine, Firewords, Bending Genres, and others. She is based between Rome and Milan. She tweets as @nanopausa. More of her words on www.nanopausa.com

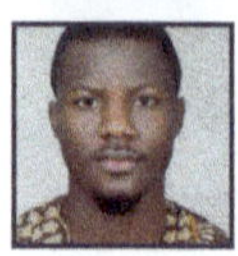

Babatunde Waliyullah Adesokan (Toonday) writes from Oyo State, Nigeria. He works with Firstbank. He is a lover of poetry; a lover of everything that breathes poetry. His works appeared in Pangolin Review, Calamuss, the QuillS, Wales Haiku, Ethel-Zine, Moida Magazine, Shallowtales Review, Stillwater Review, RoadRunnerReview, etc.

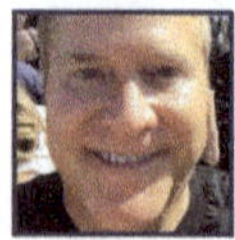

Mark Hammerschick is a lifelong resident of the Chicago area. His current work will be appearing in: Calliope, Former People Journal, Sincerely Magazine, Mignolo Arts, Blue Lake Review, Naugatuck River Review, East on Central, Grey Sparrow Journal, Griffel, Wood Cat Review, and The Rockvale Review.

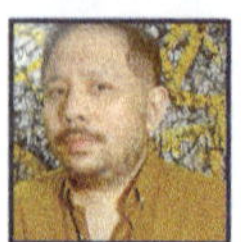

Joseph T. Salazar is a Filipino who teaches classes in Philippine and Southeast Asian Literature. He has published poems in various local publications including his own chapbook *May Laman at Mababalatan* (2005). His only published English work appears in Cha: An Asian Literary Journal.

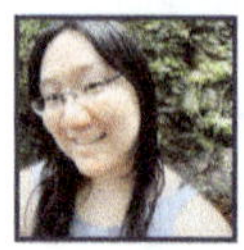

Maria S. Picone is a Korean American adoptee who won Cream City Review's 2020 Summer Poetry Prize. Her work is in Tahoma Literary Review, Seventh Wave, and Fractured Lit. She is a 2022 Palm Beach Poetry Festival Kundiman Fellow and Chestnut Review's managing editor. Her website is mariaspicone.com, Twitter @mspicone.

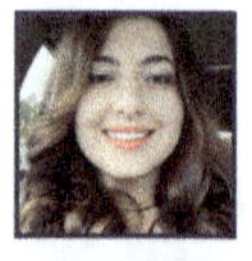

Ukrainian-born, Russian-speaking Jew, **Jane (Yevgenia!) Muschenetz** was granted asylum in the US at 10 years old. Now she is a fully-grown MIT nerd, artist, and emerging writer. Connect with Jane's work at PalmFrondZoo.com and various publications, including The San Diego Poetry Annual, Meat for Tea, and Mom Egg Review.

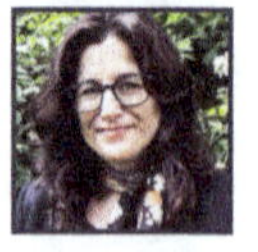

Theta Pavis lives in Jersey City. Her poetry has appeared in Spillwords, The Red Wheelbarrow, and Mom Egg Review. She teaches journalism at NJCU and spends part of each day explaining her first name (or how to pronounce it) to people, although she sometimes goes by her middle name, Reed.

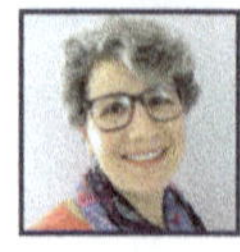

Dian Seidel is a retired climate scientist who writes and teaches in the Washington, D.C. area. She is currently working on a memoir about teaching in Thailand, excerpts of which have appeared in Passager and The New York Times. Visit her at www.DianSeidel.com.

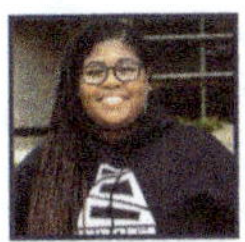

Edythe Rodriguez is a Philly-based poet who studied Africology at Temple University and loves neo-soul, battle rap, and long walks through old poetry journals. She received fellowships from The Watering Hole, Brooklyn Poets, and Palm Beach Poetry Festival. Her work is published in Obsidian, Sonku Literary Magazine, and Bayou Magazine. Her website is www.edytherodriguez.com

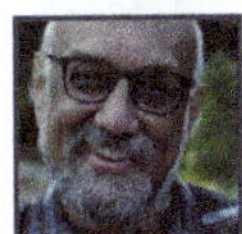

Derek Kannemeyer's books since 2019 include a play (*The Play of Gilgamesh*), a poetry collection (*Mutt Spirituals*), and a non-fiction volume (*Unsay Their Names*) about the fall from grace of Richmond's Lost Cause statuary. 50 of Unsay's photographs were the fall 2021 main exhibit at Virginia's Black History Museum.

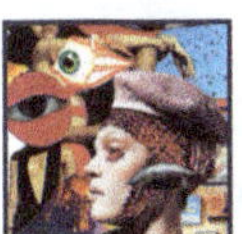

Elliott Orchard-Blowen is an artist, writer, and aspiring local hermit. He currently lives in New England, though his mind is somewhere beyond our atmosphere. You can find him at your local second-hand store, kitschy bookshop, or in the dumpsters behind a strip mall. Just knock three times on the lid.

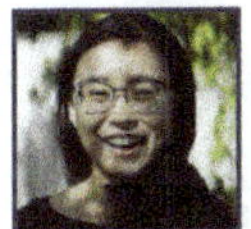

A daughter of Chinese immigrants and an immigrant herself, **Marisa Lin** (she/her) grew up in Rochester, Minnesota. Marisa began writing poems during her senior year at Stanford University, where she graduated with a BA in Economics. Marisa is an alumna of the 2021 Community of Writers Poetry Workshop.

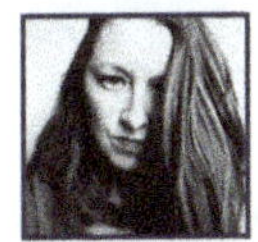

Elisabeth Mehl Greene is a writer/composer working in the DC area. She is the author of *Lady Midrash: Poems Reclaiming the Voices of Biblical Women*. Her work appears in Bourgeon, VoiceCatcher, Mizna, Journal of Feminist Studies in Religion, and the anthologies *Erase the Patriarchy* and *District Lines IV*.

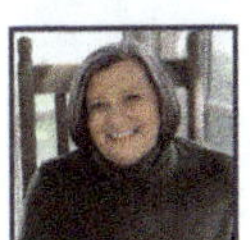

Carol Parris Krauss' poems are visual and New Southern. Her work can be found in a variety of journals such as The South Carolina Review, Story South, and Broadkill Review. She was honored to be recognized as a Best New Poet by the UVA Press. In 2021, she won the Crossroads Contest.

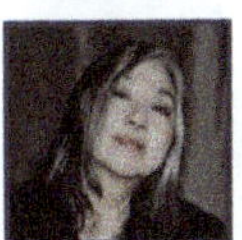

Kathleen Hellen's credits include two poetry chapbooks, *The Girl Who Loved Mothra* and *Pentimento*, and her award-winning collection *Umberto's Night*, published by Washington Writers' Publishing House. Her latest collection is *The Only Country Was the Color of My Skin*.

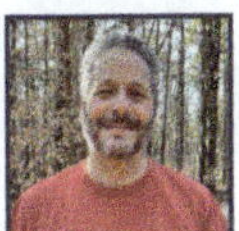

Paul Hostovsky's poems have won a Pushcart Prize, two Best of the Net Awards, and have been featured on Poetry Daily, Verse Daily, and The Writer's Almanac. He makes his living in Boston as a sign language interpreter. His latest book is MOSTLY (FutureCycle Press, 2021). Website: paulhostovsky.com

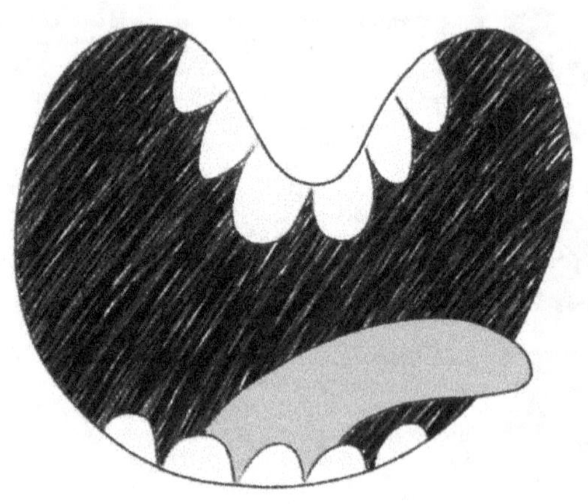

WHAT'S NEXT

Upcoming Calls For Submissions:

Sonder

Love **"Humans of New York"** or **"we're not really strangers"**? Issue 10 explores human connectivity through our own values, assumptions, and perspectives.

Poems, flash fiction, essays, hybrid forms, and art are all welcome.

Get Early Access & Submit:
May 1, 2022

FOLLOW US

 @LUCKY_JEFFERSON

 @_LUCKYJEFFERSON

 @LUCKYJEFFERSONLIT

STRIKE A POSE

TAKE A SELFIE WITH YOUR COPY OF GIBBERISH AND TAG US!

HASHTAGSSSS

USE #GIBBERISH OR #LJSQUAD TO FOLLOW THE CONVO